ABOUT THE AUTHOR

Sheena Nelson was born in Hertfordshire; she has
lived in Cornwall as well but is now living in Kent.
She has had two mental breakdowns stemming
from being abused as a child and blocking it all out.
Hypnotherapy finally released some of it but the
rest is still hidden.

Sheena has always been an avid writer of poems
and children's stories and says that writing things
down in whatever form is liberating and helps her
to get things out.

I0436486

COGS

The cogs they keep on turning
Why will they never cease
I'd like to switch them off sometimes
I'd like to have some peace.
They're grinding round my head all day
This is fine when I'm awake
But they carry on all night as well
It makes my brain cells ache.
The dreams turn into nightmares
As the crowds descend on me
I'm looking for a person
Someone I cannot see.
I wander, wander, and wander
For miles in and out
Searching for that something
I then begin to shout.
Rooms are always full
Stairs go up and down
I wander through the country
I wander through the town.
I wake up so exhausted
I can't go back to sleep
I cry with so much anguish
Then I crumple in a heap.
Why can't those cogs stop turning?
For just a little while
Why can't I have a pleasant dream?
A dream to make me smile.
I carry on through torture
No one's out there to see
I'm all alone inside my head
That's where I'll always be.

EMOTIONAL PAIN

My pain is so intense inside,
But I cannot run,
I cannot hide,
I need release, I need it now,
But I cannot get it,
I don't know how,
Turmoil runs right through my veins,
They're in my heart,
Those awful pains,
I shout, I scream in agony,
I harm, I hurt
But I'm still not free,
He torments me now,
In my dreams at night,
I sleep with the light on,
To save me from fright,
It has to come out, it's been suppressed,
But why did it stay there,
So long at rest,
Something triggered and is letting it out,
I'm not me anymore,
I'm just not about,
O help me please be rid of this pain,
Leave me in peace now,
So I can live once again.

LOST IN DRINK

I cannot think,
It goes too deep,
My mind is lost,
I cannot sleep,
Thoughts are running through my head,
Life's too short,
You're a long time dead,
I like to escape,
From reality,
It's all too much,
For me you see,
I am too deep,
I hate to think,
I like to lose myself,
In drink,
I have to face it,
Sometimes I know,
But when I drink,
I don't feel so low,
I know it's sad,
What can I say!
Perhaps I'll be able,
To face it someday,
But life's been hard,
And so am I,
Life's a bitch,
And then you die,
I just want to,
Laugh and jest,
Until I'm finally,
Laid to rest.

MIND GAMES

Translucent globules,
Of Technicolor's,
Merging into one another,
Meandering,
Beyond a dream,
Clouds of rainbows,
Of sky blue pink,
Flowers are mingling,
Rising to the suns warmth,
Multi-coloured raindrops,
Pools of wishes,
Smiles and laughter,
Memories,
My mind is altered.

NORMAL?

Who can define normality?
It's what's inside,
Not what you see,
Who first proposed?
That preposterous word?
Who shouted it out?
Who bloody well heard?
Normal is not vocabulary,
Should not be around,
In the dictionary,
It's just made trouble,
Caused a terrible storm,
And that's not right,
That's not the norm,
We're all unique,
We're not the same,
Not normal, not mad,
Just part of life's game,
So I hope whoever,
Devised that word,
Is suffering now
And not being heard.

RUNNING SCARED

I'm fleeing from an unknown thing,
An alien, a monster or myself?
Perhaps I am all three,
I know I need to run,
But how far and to where?
I stop for a while
But it never lasts,
I run again,
Always running scared,
Living on my wits,
Anxiety is high,
I cannot cope here now,
I'm off again,
It will be better then,
New place, new me,
But it never is, is it?
I'm forever running scared.

TORTURE

The torturous images,
Invade my thoughts,
I live in a nightmare,
Even in daylight,
The monsters are after me,
I try to hide,
I curl up tight
They can't get in
They're there waiting,
I cry out in anguish
Then take the pill,
Bitterness and anger
Guilt and despair
It's all calmer now.

WINDOWS OF THE SOUL

They say your eyes,
Are the windows of your soul?
So won't you look at mine?
Can you see my soul?
You should you know,
As that is all I have left,
Everything else I have given away,
To some other soul,
Everything else,
But I knew not to give them my soul,
I know that is too precious,
I have to keep it,
It's the only thing,
That keeps me going,
If I were soulless,
I would just be a body,
I couldn't do that,
Everything else has gone now,
Everything else,
All I need is a light in there,
A light for my soul,
A light to spur me on,
To help me feel again,
Everything else has gone now,
Everything,

But my soul lingers on,
Ever in hope.

ABUSE

He will come and get me
He will do it again
He is nasty
I didn't know
But I knew it was wrong
I felt sick
I promised him
I won't tell
He will come for me
If I tell
He will come
It will be worse
He will hurt me
As well as touch me
He will make me bleed
He said so
It's my secret
I run now
When I see big men
With their shirts
Their jumpers tucked in
A belt that can hurt
A fat tummy
Nasty man
I have nightmares
I want to speak
I'm not allowed
He will know
Then he stopped
I saw him no more
But he hasn't gone
He will never leave
He is in my head
Along with my secret
And I cannot speak.

DESTINATION UNKNOWN

I'm sitting in the doorway now,
Feeling so alone,
I do not know what's happening,
My destination is unknown,
My thoughts they keep on travelling,
But I do not know to where,
My mind is still so muddled,
What's going on in there?
I'm sitting in the doorway now,
Looking down that long dark road,
That is where I'm going,
On my back is a heavy load,
And still I cannot shift it,
It won't lighten so what do I do?
The road is forever winding,
I don't think I can get through,
I'm sitting in the doorway now,
Feeling so alone,
I do not know what's happening,
My destination is unknown,
There must be someone out there,
Someone to give me a lift,
To tell me where I'm heading,
To get that load to shift,
Somebody that will take me,
Where I need to go,
Someone who will be with me,
To help me find a place I know,
I'm sitting in the doorway now,
Feeling so alone,
I do not know what's happening,
My destination is unknown.

IN THE CLINIC

Never be a cynic,
Until you've been inside the clinic,
Never be a Judge,
Until you've had that nudge,
Never tease or bully,
Until you know somebody fully,
Never mention madness,
Until you've been through certain sadness,
Never think you're better,
Until you've led life to the letter,
Never say 'a nutter',
Until you've been down in the gutter,
Never criticise,
Until you open both your eyes,
Never say 'not me',
Until you know what you can be,
Never think you're clever,
Until you know you're safe forever.

MANIA

My brain is confused,
It doesn't know which way to go,
My wires are crossed,
The signals are tapping S.O.S.
My nerve endings are on fire
Fight or flight?
Run, run away from it
But it follows,
Fight it, fight it,
But it wins,
Hyper, everything is hyper,
My body wants to rush,
But it also panics; I'm not in control,
The mania is coming.

MIND

Mind, a complex muscle
Some are travesties
Not wired up right
Not all there
Mental!
Mind
A tangle of machinery
All working together
Some have bits missing
But there's no engineer
They try to be
Try to weld up those loose wires
They say it's all fixed
Cowboy workers
Feels OK for a while
But never complete
Mind
We shall never know the truth.

OFFENCE (TO GOD)

Why do you point that dagger,
Always towards my heart?
I am not the one, who has wronged you,
Or anyone else,
I have struggled,
Been strangled and felt the intense pain,
But always I have survived,
Why then do you still do this?
Why not now let me free?
I have suffered enough,
And pointing that sword will not help,
It torments me more,
But it will not pierce,
Not yet
I will still try to break through,
I will blunt your sharpness,
For you have not just offended me,
You have offended my soul.

THE DREAM COUNCIL

How complex a mind is?
A labyrinth of thoughts,
Pictures, dreams, nightmares,
All hidden,
All waiting,
Waiting to emerge,
Just when you are tired,
When all you want to do,
Is sleep peacefully,
Where does it all come from?
All these images,
They all appear,
Round in circles,
From deep in your subconscious,
To right behind,
Your eyelids,
Like a badly made film,
But I do escape eventually,
I struggle free,
Then lay there,
Too scared to close,
My eyes again,
I know they are waiting.

VISIONS

I have visions,
Though not of a psychic,
I have visions,
Of nightmares,
In opiate dreams,
Visions of people,
I knew or know,
Visions of places,
Many places,
I talk, I walk,
I run, I fly,
I kiss, I hug,
I have sex, I cry,
Always people,
In crisis,
In trouble,
In my mind,
In a bubble,
Being kind,
I have visions,
Of the past,
Of the present,
Never of the future,
So much has passed,
So much in my head,
Tangles, knots,
Stickiness, lots,
Rushing, pouring,
Gushing, soaring,
Always on the go,
Visions of my life,
Visions of pain.

BRAIN

Brain, in pain,
A tangled ball of wool,
Knots there's lots,
Mush, yes a swirling pool.
Brain, a strain,
Muscles pulled so tight,
Parts like darts,
Stabbing with such might.
Brain, insane,
Mental, labelled me,
Scare, not fair,
You, you cannot see.
Brain, like rain,
Drips my tortured soul,
Mend it, send,
A drill to make a hole.
Brain, a stain,
A blot of madness now,
Sad, not bad,
Nobody knows how
Brain, a drain,
Down the pipe it goes,
Flush, a rush,
Now it really shows.

Brain, no gain,
No cure out there at all,
Drugs, you mugs,
I'm up against a wall.
Brain, in vain,
Not enough is known,
Health needs wealth,
The coffers all have flown.

DO YOU?

Which way should you look at life?
Which way should you turn your head?
Do you stand there sometimes and ponder?
Do you think you'd be better off dead?
Do you force yourself to struggle?
Do you drag yourself through life?
Do you long for the happier moments?
Do you try not to think of the strife?
Do you try to make ends meet?
Do you wonder if it's worth all the pain?
Do you sit down and cry with anguish?
Do you get up and try once again?
Which way do you look at life?
Which way should you turn your head?
Do any of you know the answer?
Do any of you care what I said?

LOBOTOMY

Oh if it were only true
A lobotomy on me to do
To get into that intricate maze
Which to me is a total haze
A mist that I cannot get through
No matter what I try to do
Is there no one here to clear the fog?
To stop me looking so agog
To rearrange the cells that be
Totally confusing me
When life rears its ugly head
I just want to stay in bed
It's safer there for my head you see
While I wait for that frontal lobotomy
Rattle my brains, shake them about
To stop me wanting to scream and shout
Put plasters on the bits that are cut
Sew up my head with strong cat gut
Then at peace at last I'll be
Cured by my lobotomy.

MAYBE

Does the past ever cling to you?
Like a prickly blanket?
You can't move on,
Or face the future,
Maybe there is no,
Future,
Maybe the past,
Will be the future,
Or maybe, just maybe,
The future will,
Erase the past,
The blanket will,
Become soft,
You can move again.

NATURE OF THE MIND
Go walk among the trees,
The fields
The lakes or rivers
Go stroll along country lanes
Through grasses
Over hills
Go breathe in the sweet air
The smell of mown grass
The scent of wild flowers
Go run across a meadow
Feel the freedom
Feel the spirit
Go sit among nature
Stop for a while
Stare for a while
Go and get some nature in your mind
Look around you
Let it in
Let it soak into your head
Feel hope
Feel
The nature of your mind.

PAIN

Pain is there every day,
All over me,
Come what may,
It's physical,
It's mental too,
I'm so distraught,
What can I do?
I struggle on,
I try to be,
What once I was,
The old me,
Sometimes though,
I have to give in,
I cannot move,
I cannot win,
Then I ask,
The question why,
I cast my eyes,
Up to the sky,
The answer though,
To hear my prayer,
Is not about
Is never there,
There is no cure,
It just won't go,
You cannot see it,
It doesn't show,
So how can I,
Explain it all?
I'm hitting my head,
Against a brick wall,
But I'm hoping one day,
I will get release,
And maybe then,
My pain will cease.

THOUGHTS WHILE FLOATING

I'm floating along on a pink mushroom cloud,
Where butterflies are flying,
And silence is loud,
All I can hear is the song of the dove,
All I can see are the stars up above,
Where war and peace are mixed together,
I know somehow it won't last forever,
I know one day the devil will arise,
Down from below, up into the skies,
I know that then my world will end,
With the evil and torture he will send,
I know then too no longer will I,
Be floating along on this cloud in the sky.

WAITING GAME

It's a waiting game I play,
With my mind,
As it is this way
I wait for it to implode
I know it's on
Overload
Hyper, manic
High
My mind won't
Stop
Though I try
Buzzing bumble
Bee
It's all tangled up
You see
It's a waiting game I play
With my mind
As it is this way
I want now
To be calm
I hope I won't
Come to harm
Then as quick it
Goes
But it keeps me
On my toes
This waiting game I
Play
This waiting game
Of brain
As my brain it is
This way.